W9-BNA-046

THOMAS "STONEWALL" JACKSON

CONFEDERATE GENERAL

SPECIAL LIVES IN HISTORY THAT BECOME

Signature LIVES

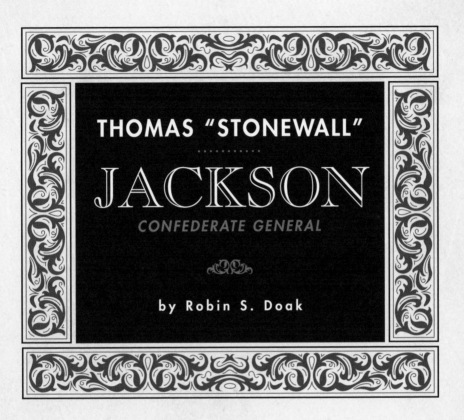

THOMAS "STONEWALL"
JACKSON
CONFEDERATE GENERAL

by Robin S. Doak

Content Adviser: Babs Melton,
Director, Stonewall Jackson Museum,
Strasburg, Virginia

Reading Adviser: Rosemary G. Palmer, Ph.D.,
Department of Literacy, College of Education,
Boise State University

COMPASS POINT BOOKS  MINNEAPOLIS, MINNESOTA

Compass Point Books
3109 West 50th Street, #115
Minneapolis, MN 55410

Visit Compass Point Books on the Internet at *www.compasspointbooks.com*
or e-mail your request to *custserv@compasspointbooks.com*

Editor: Editorial Directions, Inc.
Lead Designer: Jaime Martens
Photo Researcher: Marcie C. Spence
Page Production: Jaime Martens, Bobbie Nuytten
Cartographer: XNR Productions, Inc.
Educational Consultant: Diane Smolinski

Managing Editor: Catherine Neitge
Creative Director: Keith Griffin
Editorial Director: Carol Jones

Library of Congress Cataloging-in-Publication Data
Doak, Robin S. (Robin Santos), 1963–
   Thomas "Stonewall" Jackson : Confederate general / by Robin S. Doak.
      p. cm.—(Signature lives)
   Includes bibliographical references and index.
   ISBN 0-7565-0987-4 (hard cover)
   1. Jackson, Stonewall, 1824–1863—Juvenile literature. 2. Generals—
Confederate States of America—Biography—Juvenile literature.
3. Confederate States of America. Arm—Biography—Juvenile literature.
4. United States—History—Civil War, 1861–1865—Campaigns—Juvenile
literature. I. Title. II. Series.
E467.1.J15D63 2006
973.7'42'092—dc22   2005002789

© 2006 by Compass Point Books
All rights reserved. No part of this book may be reproduced without written permission
from the publisher. The publisher takes no responsibility for the use of any of the
materials or methods described in this book, nor for the products thereof.
Printed in the United States of America.

Signature Lives

CIVIL WAR ERA

The Civil War (1861–1865) split the United States into two countries and divided the people over the issue of slavery. The opposing sides—the Union in the North and the Confederacy in the South—battled each other for four long years in the deadliest American conflict ever fought. The bloody war sometimes pitted family members and friends against each other over the issues of slavery and states' rights. Some of the people who lived and served their country during the Civil War are among the nation's most beloved heroes.

Table of Contents

1 DARK DAYS

Chapter

୧ৎ⌇ও৶

On a hot July day in the summer of 1861, the battle near Manassas Junction, Virginia, was not going well for the Southern troops. Although Confederates out-numbered Union forces, they were tired and untrained and were being beaten on their own land. Union supporters expected that the battle would be the first and last of the Civil War. Many had traveled 30 miles (48 kilometers) from Washington, D.C., to witness the skirmish. Men dressed in fine suits and women in fancy dresses lined up on a hill near Bull Run to watch the fighting.

Despite the odds against him, Confederate General Thomas Jackson refused to give up. He ordered his men to form and hold a long line in front of the enemy troops. The men obeyed, standing bravely and waiting for the Northern attack to come.

The sight was an inspiration to other Southern soldiers. A general from South Carolina pointed to Jackson and shouted, "Look! There is Jackson standing like a stone wall! Rally behind the Virginians!" By the end of that day, Union troops were driven from the battlefield in defeat in the First Battle of Bull Run. And the legend known as "Stonewall" Jackson was born and became an important symbol for the Confederate cause.

Tension between the North and South built quickly after Abraham Lincoln was elected president. States in the South began to secede, or withdraw, from the Union. In December 1860, South Carolina became the first state to leave. On February 4, 1861, South Carolina and six other states formed a new independent nation called the Confederate States of America. Jefferson Davis of Mississippi was elected its first president.

The spring of 1861 marked the start of the darkest days in U.S. history. In April, the battle over

The Civil War began on April 12, 1861, when Confederate troops fired on Fort Sumter, a U.S. military outpost in Charleston, South Carolina. The war ended four long years later, when Confederate General Robert E. Lee surrendered to Union General Ulysses S. Grant at Appomattox Court House in Virginia. The Civil War remains the bloodiest episode in U.S. history. More Americans died during the conflict than in any other war.

Abraham Lincoln was elected the 16th president of the United States in 1860. He served as president until 1865, when he was assassinated.

slavery and states' rights had ripped America in two, separating North from South. For years, many people in the North had wanted to end slavery in the United States. They were called abolitionists. People

The largest sculpture of Thomas "Stonewall" Jackson is at Stone Mountain Park near Atlanta, Georgia. The figures on horseback of Robert E. Lee, Jefferson Davis, and Jackson are carved into the mountainside. The sculpture is a relief, which means the figures stand out from a flat background. It is 400 feet (122 meters) above the ground and measures 90 feet (27 m) by 100 feet (30 m) in size. The carved area covers about 3 acres (1.2 hectares).

in the South had worked just as hard to preserve their rights and way of life, which included owning slaves.

When the country split in two, Thomas "Stonewall" Jackson was one of many Virginians who remained loyal to his state and the South. Jackson fought not to preserve slavery, but to preserve Virginia's rights to self-government. In June 1862, he wrote to his wife Anna, "How I do wish for peace, but only upon the condition of our national independence."

Jackson became known as one of the greatest leaders and most skillful commanders of the Civil War. He defeated Union troops much larger than his own and turned certain defeats into victories. General Robert E. Lee, commander of the Confederate Army, relied heavily on Jackson, calling him his best general and his right arm.

Jackson was one of the first military heroes of the war. Many of his men believed that he was unbeatable. Just the sight of the general on horse-

back caused rebel soldiers to burst into cheers. Jackson was a hero to all Southerners and served as an inspiration during the war.

Jackson achieved his greatest fame in the final two years of his life. Unfortunately, he was killed during the war at the height of his career. Many believe that his death sealed the fate of the South.

The relief sculpture at Stone Mountain Park near Atlanta, Georgia, is the largest in the world. Work on the carving began in 1915 and was completed in 1972.

2 OVERCOMING MISFORTUNE

❧

Thomas Jackson was born on January 21, 1824, in the little frontier town of Clarksburg in what is now West Virginia. He was the third Jackson child. Thomas' father, Jonathan, was a lawyer in the area. Although intelligent and likable, the elder Jackson was fond of gambling and had trouble paying his bills. He struggled to support his growing family. Thomas' mother, Julia, was the daughter of a prosperous Virginia merchant.

In 1826, Thomas' oldest sister, Elizabeth, died of typhoid fever. Two weeks later, their father died of the same disease. The next day, Thomas' mother gave birth to a daughter, Laura. Over the years, Laura would prove to be Thomas' one nearly constant companion.

Thomas and his siblings were born in a frontier town in the early 1800s. At that time, much of present-day America was still relatively unsettled.

When he died, Jonathan Jackson left his wife and children penniless. Thomas' mother was forced to sell the family's home to pay off his debts. In 1830, she remarried, but her new husband was unkind to the children. He even told them to "seek homes elsewhere."

In 1831, Julia Jackson decided that her children would be better off living with relatives. Thomas' older brother Warren was sent to live with his mother's family. Seven-year-old Thomas and 5-year-old Laura were sent to live with their father's relatives in Jackson's Mill in what is now West Virginia. The town was founded in 1801 by Thomas' grandfather, Edward Jackson.

Jonathan Jackson, Stonewall Jackson's father

Being separated from his mother deeply affected Thomas. Even as an adult, it was one of his most painful memories. But just three months after leaving, Thomas and Laura were called back home. Their mother was dying after giving birth to a son, William, and she wanted to see her children one last time.

Thomas and Laura's childhood home in Jackson's Mill

After her death, Thomas and Laura returned to Jackson's Mill, where they lived with their Uncle Cummins Jackson. He was a well-to-do businessman and a leading member of the Jackson's Mill community. He owned two mills, a carpenter's shop, a general store, and other property.

Thomas lived with his uncle until he was 18. During this time, he worked in the mill and labored side by side with his uncle's slaves. He also tended the family's crops and farm animals and did other tasks and odd jobs. For fun, Thomas hunted, fished,

17

and rode horses. He even served as his uncle's jockey in horse races. Many years later, after hearing about Cummins' death in 1850, Jackson wrote, "This is news which goes to my heart; uncle was a father to me."

Growing up with his hardworking uncle, Thomas had little time to go to school. After his uncle established a school for boys at his mill, Thomas took every opportunity to get an education. Although schooling did not come easily to him, he was fiercely determined. A childhood friend later said that Thomas was "not what is nowadays termed brilliant, but he was one of those untiring, matter-of-fact persons who would never give up an undertaking until he accomplished his object."

When Thomas was 16, his reputation of being honest, responsible, and hardworking earned him his first paying job as a schoolteacher. He earned $5.64 for three months of work. He later served as county constable, a type of sheriff. During Thomas' 10-month job as the constable, his 20-year-old brother Warren died of tuberculosis. Now, only he, his sister, Laura, and their half-brother, William, remained.

In 1841, Thomas learned that a local congressman was interviewing candidates for an opening at the U.S. Military Academy at West Point in New York. The academy, founded in 1802, was a school to train young men to become U.S. Army officers. After taking a series of tests, an acquaintance of Thomas' got the appointment. Thomas was very disappointed, but he soon received good news. After one day in the tough military environment, his friend packed his bags and left West Point. Thomas was admitted to the academy.

At West Point, Thomas started off slowly. In a class of 101 cadets, he finished 51st after his first year. But he was determined to do better. Although he had less schooling than the other cadets, he worked twice as hard. Thomas studied day and

President Thomas Jefferson signed legislation establishing West Point in 1802.

During his four years at West Point, Thomas studied many different subjects. They included algebra, geometry, logic, ethics, engineering, French, history, chemistry, and drawing. West Point cadets also practiced marching in step, horseback riding, and fencing.

night, hitting the books by candlelight when the sun went down. He quickly earned a reputation among his classmates as a hard worker—and a very sweaty one. A classmate later recalled, "In his mental efforts ... great drops of perspiration would roll from his face, even in the coldest weather."

Although Thomas was not the most popular student at West Point, he was admired by the other cadets. A classmate later remembered going to school with Thomas:

> While there were many who seemed to surpass him in intellect, in geniality, and in good-fellowship, there was no one of our class who more absolutely possessed the respect and confidence of all. And in the end "Old Jack," as he was always called ... came to be regarded by his comrades with something very like affection.

While he was at the academy, Thomas began keeping a notebook with phrases of inspiration and encouragement. He collected ideas from books he had read and wrote down the phrases that meant the most to him. One of his favorite sayings was "You may be whatever you will resolve to be." Others were, "Endeavor to be at peace with all men" and "Sacrifice your life rather than your word." Thomas also wrote encouraging letters to his sister, Laura. In one letter he advised, "Be not discouraged by disappointments and difficulties but on the contrary let each stimulate you to greater exertions in attaining noble ends."

By the end of his second year, Thomas had moved up to 30th in his class; the following year, he

Thomas was a very determined student at West Point.

> *Many famous Civil War figures graduated from West Point, including Jefferson Davis, Robert E. Lee, William Tecumseh Sherman, and Ulysses S. Grant.*

rose to 20th. John Esten Cooke, a man who fought for the Confederacy and later wrote about Jackson, talked about Thomas' drive to succeed at West Point. Cooke wrote, "He did not penetrate the subject before him at a glance, but mastered it by laborious application. ... What he once acquired was drilled into his mind, and every step which he ascended was solid under his feet."

In the summer of 1846, Thomas Jackson graduated from West Point. His final ranking was 17th in a class of 59 students. Many of his classmates believed that if Thomas had one more year of study, he would have finished first in his class.

In May 1846, the United States declared war on Mexico. The Mexican War had been brewing for many years. In 1835, American settlers living in Texas had risen up against Mexican rule. The following year, they won their independence and proclaimed the Republic of Texas. Texas was annexed by the United States in 1845, becoming the 28th U.S. state. After Texas was annexed, Mexico broke off diplomatic relations with the United States.

The war between the United States and Mexico also resulted from a dispute over the boundary

between the two countries. The United States claimed all the land north of the Rio Grande. Mexico, however, claimed that the border was the Nueces River, near Corpus Christi, Texas. After graduation, Thomas and his classmates waited eagerly for their assignments. Many of the cadets wanted to head south into the excitement of battle. Thomas was thrilled when he was commissioned as a second lieutenant in the 1st Artillery Regiment. He eagerly left New York and traveled to meet his regiment in Mexico. ℘

Thomas was eager to prove his skills as a soldier during the Mexican War.

3 ARMY LIFE

❧

The Mexican War was raging when 22-year-old Thomas Jackson arrived in Texas in September 1846. The following month, he moved into Mexico to join his regiment and waited to see action. His first battle experience came in March 1847 during an attack on the city of Veracruz. Jackson's artillery unit bombarded the city until the Mexicans surrendered.

Jackson quickly earned a reputation for his bravery, quick thinking, and ability to remain calm and make decisions even when under fire. After his regiment fought battles at Contreras and Churubusco, Jackson's commanding officer praised his skills: "If devotion, industry, talent, and gallantry are the highest qualities of a soldier, then he is enti-

During the Mexican War, Jackson fought in the Battle of Chapultepec.

tled to the distinction which their profession [gives them]." Jackson was soon promoted to first lieutenant.

Jackson again proved his abilities at the Battle of Chapultepec. During the heat of battle, his men lost their nerve and deserted their guns. Although frightened himself, Jackson strode up and down by the guns, saying, "See, there is no danger; I am not hit!" Jackson later confided that it was the only time he ever intentionally lied to anyone. While trying to convince his men to take their positions, a Mexican cannonball passed between his legs. Jackson still held his ground. After the battle, word spread that the young officer was unbeatable.

After displaying bravery and strong leadership skills at Chapultepec, Jackson was promoted to brevet major.

As a result of his bravery and leadership skills, Jackson was soon promoted to the rank of brevet major. In less than a year, he had been promoted twice. No one who had graduated with him from West Point performed as well or was promoted as rapidly.

The war also gave Jackson valuable firsthand experience in battlefield tactics and dealing with soldiers. Jackson loved life on the battle-field, and he developed his own ideas about being an effective leader.

When the war ended in 1847, Jackson was assigned to General Winfield Scott's forces occupying Mexico City. During his nine months there, the young officer had the chance to enjoy Mexico City and meet the residents. Jackson and his fellow soldiers were treated kindly by the Mexicans and often took part in local festivities. In Mexico, Jackson learned how to dance. He also studied Spanish so that he could better converse with the people there. By the time he left Mexico, he had learned enough of the language to read several Spanish books, including a history of Mexico. Jackson also talked to Mexican priests about the Roman Catholic religion, the main religion of Mexico.

While in Mexico, Jackson often wrote to his sister, Laura. In one letter, Jackson's loneliness and concern for Laura are obvious:

> *The Mexican War officially ended on February 2, 1848, when the United States and Mexico signed a peace treaty. Under the terms of the treaty, the United States gained more than 525,000 square miles (1,365,000 sq km) of land. The new land included all of present-day California, Nevada, and Utah, as well as parts of Arizona and New Mexico. In return, the United States agreed to pay $15 million for the new land.*

As three successive mails have arrived, without bringing a single letter from you, I am (and I think not without reason) uneasy about your health. As I do not know of any other reason but bad health which could have prevented your writing to a brother who is interested in everything that interests you. And I hope that if you have any regard for my peace of mind that you will write at least once every fortnight. If your health forbids your writing at any time, then get some-one to write for you, if it should be but a dozen lines. I do not think that a regular mail has left this city, without carrying a letter for you from me.

Jackson and his sister, Laura, corresponded while he was stationed in Mexico City.

In Mexico City, Jackson met a young woman in whom he grew very interested. He even considered remaining in Mexico. In the end, however, Jackson chose to leave the country in June 1848 with the rest of the U.S. troops.

In July 1848, Jackson was assigned to Fort Hamilton, just a few miles from

New York City. With the country at peace, the young man had the spare time available to pursue some of his favorite activities. In New York, he had access to bookstores and public libraries. Jackson promised himself that he would read at least 40 pages a day. He was especially interested in religion, politics, and history. When he died years later, he left behind a personal library that included biographies, history books, Shakespeare's works, and books in five different languages.

In New York, Jackson became very religious. He began reading the Bible every day, and attended services at Methodist, Baptist, Episcopalian, and Roman Catholic churches, looking for a religion that was right for him.

Jackson's views on religion were sometimes related to his physical ailments. At West Point, Jackson had begun to suffer from indigestion problems. In New York, Jackson had visited a number of doctors, but they had failed to help him. He now

> *Jackson believed that pure water could cure just about every illness or physical complaint. When Laura complained about achy eyes, he offered the following suggestion: "I wish you would try the simple remedy of washing them with cold water, lifting the water to the face in both hands and washing the face until a little water gets into the eyes and they commence smarting. Do this at night just before going to bed, and again immediately after getting up."*

A view of Fort Hamilton during the 1800s

believed that these ailments were punishment for his sins. Later in life, Jackson was troubled with poor eyesight, deafness, and cold feet. He watched his diet and visited spas for water therapy treatments. In later years, he purchased equipment that allowed him to exercise at home. For the rest of his life, Jackson was vigilant about taking good care of himself.

Despite his health concerns, Jackson found time to have fun in New York City. In letters to Laura, he described attending parties and going on sleigh rides. He wrote of the "very many interesting young ladies" he met while at Fort Hamilton. Jackson spent two years in New York and came to like the city very much. In April 1849, he wrote to Laura:

> *In New York may be found all most any-thing which the inclinations may desire; but peaceful quiet: every thing is in motion, every thing is alive with anima-tion. In its busy throng, none feel the long tedious hour; even the invalid for the time forgets his infirmities, and with wonder-ing animation contemplates the sur-rounding scene.*

Although his career in the military had only just begun, Jackson's world had expanded. He had visited Mexico, New York, and other places, and he found them to his liking. He had also learned to enjoy his free time. Finally, Jackson had discovered that a soldier's life agreed with him. ℘

Chapter 4

A New Career

⧬⧬⧬

In 1850, Jackson's company was sent to Fort Meade in Florida to protect settlers from the Seminole Indians. The Seminoles had been fighting since 1817 to keep their land. Although the warm weather agreed with Jackson, he soon became bored. After enjoying the social and cultural opportunities of New York City, Jackson quickly decided that the wilderness of Florida—especially during peacetime—was not the place for him.

Fort Meade was a tiny outpost in the middle of a wild, swampy area. The nearest settlement was more than 10 miles (16 km) away. Only a year old, the fort itself was made up of several wooden buildings that had been hastily erected, including a storehouse and a hospital. Enlisted men slept in one

Thomas Jackson as a young soldier

building, and officers bunked in another. The commanding officer got his own log cabin.

Each day's routine was much the same. The men arose 30 minutes before sunrise. After roll call, each man groomed his horse for 20 minutes. Breakfast followed, with lunch at noon. Soldiers guarded the fort in two shifts, the first beginning at 9 A.M., the

During his lifetime, Thomas Jackson lived in the South, along the East Coast, and even in Mexico.

second at 4:30 P.M. Lights out was at 8:45 P.M. For the men, an exciting day consisted of the occasional scouting mission into the Florida wilds.

Jackson soon found himself at odds with his commander, Captain William French. He was a strict, aggressive man who insulted his officers and severely disciplined his troops. The commander angered Jackson by criticizing him and taking away some of his responsibilities. In addition, Jackson had heard rumors that French was mistreating his wife, a woman who had become a good friend to Jackson. When Jackson took it upon himself to investigate the rumors, French had him arrested. In turn, Jackson filed charges against his commander. The affair ended when superior officers told both French and Jackson to forget the matter. After spending more than a month under arrest, Jackson was finally released on May 16, 1851.

Just four days later, Jackson left the Army to become professor of natural and experimental

Jackson's physical appearance was unremarkable—except for his piercing, pale gray-blue eyes. Another instructor at Virginia Military Institute described him as fairly ordinary looking: "There was nothing striking about his exterior. ... His figure was large-boned, angular and even ungainly for his hands and especially his feet were very large. He had a heavy, ungraceful and lumbering walk, altogether different from the springy regular and soldier-like gait which is produced by early military training."

philosophy at the Virginia Military Institute (VMI) in Lexington, Virginia. The course covered physics, astronomy, optics, and other topics that Jackson knew little about. He was also an artillery instructor, a job that suited him much better.

Founded in 1839, VMI was created to educate and prepare young men for military service. When Jackson signed on as an instructor, the institute had just five faculty members.

Like everything else that he did, Jackson took teaching very seriously. With his strict rules and inflexible set of morals, the new professor was disliked by his students. He was boring, talked as little

Virginia Military Institute is the oldest state-supported military school in the United States.

as possible, and rarely laughed. Later, Jackson's superior at the institute wrote, "He was no teacher, and he lacked the tact required in getting along with his classes."

The boys at VMI found plenty of nicknames for their new instructor, including "Deacon Jackson," "Old Jack," "Tom Fool," "Old Blue Light," and "Square Box," an insult aimed at his big feet. Jackson was also the target of many practical jokes and pranks. Students drew huge pictures of feet on his chalkboard and marched behind him when he wasn't looking, imitating his long, stiff stride. Jackson was such an unpopular teacher that a group of former students attempted—unsuccessfully—to get him fired.

In 1855, Jackson founded a Sunday school for black children, even though this was against the law and customs of the time. In 1858, he reported that 91 pupils attended the school.

Some of Jackson's students had feelings that ran even stronger than mere dislike. A senior cadet named James A. Walker was expelled a few weeks before graduation after Jackson reported that he had behaved disrespectfully in class. A furious Walker challenged his former teacher to a duel. The duel was prevented when the cadet's father arrived at the institute to take his son home. Walker would later serve as a colonel under Jackson.

While teaching at VMI, Jackson chose a religion to practice. Although he had been baptized an Episcopalian in 1849, he began attending Lexington's Presbyterian Church. Jackson was attracted to the intelligent sermons he heard there and attended every church service.

During Jackson's 10 years in Lexington, religion became very important to him. He refused to do anything on Sundays, including working, writing letters, or reading the paper. He vowed not to drink, smoke, or gamble, and he prayed at every opportunity. Jackson once said:

> *I have so fixed the habit in my own mind that I never raise a glass of water to my lips without a moment's asking of God's blessing. I never seal a letter without putting a word of prayer under the seal. I never take a letter from the post without a brief sending of my thoughts heavenward.*

Jackson loved his adopted town of Lexington. He wrote, "Of all the places that have come under my observation in the United States, this little village is the most beautiful." Jackson made the most of his weekends and vacation time in Lexington. He pursued his interest in art and culture and continued to add books—mostly religious—to his library. He also planted a garden.

Jackson liked the townspeople, too, especially a young woman named Elinor Junkin. "Ellie," as Jackson called her, was the daughter of the president of Washington College in Lexington. In the summer of 1853, the two married. Jackson adored his new wife, writing to his sister that Ellie was a "great source of happiness." This happiness didn't last long, however. Ellie died just 14 months after their marriage while giving birth. The couple's son was not alive when he was born. Their deaths shattered Jackson. He wrote to an old classmate, "I desire no more days on Earth."

In an effort to escape his grief, Jackson traveled to Europe in July 1856. He visited England, Scotland, Belgium, France, Germany, Switzerland, and Italy. He returned to the United States in October with a new outlook on life and a desire to find another wife.

Jackson's search didn't last long. In 1857, he married Mary Anna Morrison of North Carolina. Like Jackson's first wife, Anna was the daughter of a former college president and

Elinor "Ellie" Junkin was Jackson's first wife. She died during childbirth 14 months after their wedding.

Mary Anna Morrison was Jackson's second wife.

Presbyterian minister. Jackson had known Anna for several years. When he returned from his European adventure, he began writing to her. Anna later recalled the first letter, "expressing such blissful memories ... of the summer we had been together in Lexington that my sister Eugenia laughed most heartily over it and predicted an early visit from the major." In April 1858, their first child—a daughter named Mary—was born. Sadly, the infant lived less than a month. In November 1862, the couple would have another child, a daughter named Julia Laura. She was born while her father was away at war.

Jackson's home life with Anna was a happy one. Anna described her husband dancing the polka and playacting with her. His happiness increased when his nephew Thomas—his beloved sister Laura's son—came to Lexington to attend school. Jackson was so affectionate toward his nephew that he didn't want to be the one to correct the boy's mistakes. He wrote to his sister:

[Thomas] has contracted another very bad habit of working his upper lip and nose by means of the muscles. He also picks his nose instead of blowing it. I wish you would write to him about these habits and tell him to let his nose and lip remain at rest and to blow his nose hard until he gets it clean and then let it alone. I have talked to him upon the subject and I think that he has improved some. But it is very unpleasant to have to say such things to him as are calculated to wound his feelings.

Jackson's quiet and contentment wouldn't last long. National events would soon disturb his happy home, and he would find himself playing an important role in the coming drama. ❧

FRANK LESLIE'S ILLUSTRATED NEWS PAPER

Entered according to Act of Congress in the year 1859, by FRANK LESLIE, in the Clerk's Office of the District Court for the Southern District of New York.

No. 207.—VOL. VIII.   NEW YORK, SATURDAY, NOVEMBER 19, 1859.   [PRICE 6 CENTS.

THE HARPER'S FERRY INSURRECTION.
JOHN BROWN

WE give in our present number a likeness of the arch-conspirator, which admirably portrays that stern and deluded man. As we published in No. 205 a short biography of him, we shall content ourselves now with saying that his second wife is living at Port Elba, with three of their children, of which two are daughters. She is described as a very respectable woman, and deeply feels the dangerous position of her misguided husband. She passed through this city on her way to Charlestown, to visit him, one day last week.

It would seem from the statement of the *Herald of Freedom*, a Kansas paper, that Brown was famous during his short career there for his passion for fighting, and that he was more fitted for the days of Hotspur and Douglas than for the nineteenth century. The editor of that paper accuses him of many terrible crimes, the chief of which is the murder of eight unoffending citizens, who were roused from their beds, in May, 1856, and deliberately murdered within gunshot of their dwellings.

Redpath, one of the Kansas agitators, denies the statement that Brown was concerned in this outrage, and while admitting the fact of the massacre, attributes it to other parties. There can, however, be no question that the conduct of Ossawattamie Brown was of the most violent character, and on a par with that of the Border Ruffians.

The Southern press also denies most energetically that the wrongs sustained by Brown were the cause of his bitter hostility to the slaveholders. It was, from first to last, his fanatical hatred of the institution. This feeling was confirmed by the openly avowed doctrines of great orators like Beecher and Cheever, and the passive approbation of such distinguished men as Greeley, Seward and their clique.

There is one peculiarity in John Brown which belongs more to the gloomy Covenanter than the American farmer—thus he brought up his sons, if we may judge from the diary kept by one of those unhappy young men, in a state of patriarchal reverence of him, as the head of the family. He also rebukes one for swearing, and urges another to pray.

In fact, John Brown, a traitor to the American Union, would have been a patriot by the side of Oliver Cromwell. He was miserably unfitted to the age in which he lived, and will pay the penalty for his untameable and headstrong nature.

We conclude with some anecdotes exemplifying his indomitable will, which, as they are taken from the *Tribune*, we presume may be received as authentic.

A committee of five called on him on one occasion, and informed him that he must leave the Territory in three days, or die—that they would come to his house with a sufficient force at the end of that time, and if they found him still here they would hang him. The old man thanked them for the notice, saying, very coolly, "You will not find me here then, gentlemen." Before the next sun rose the five members of that committee were in the other world. Whether Brown killed them or not is unknown, but it is certain, had they lived, that they would have killed him, and no man knew that better than he. On one occasion the well-known Henry Clay Pate started out from Westport, Missouri, with a party of thirty-three men, full of boastings and promises to catch "Old Brown" and take him a prisoner to Missouri, his only fear being that he would not be able to find him. Brown was very easily found, however, for with sixteen men he went out to meet Pate, and after a short fight with a f— men killed and wounded, at Black-Jack, near the Santa Fé ro— Pate and his party surrendered to "Old Brown," with the exception of a Wyandot Indian by the name of Long, and the notorious Colen— who had murdered Dow. These two men, being well mounted, ma— their escape.

JOHN BROWN, NOW UNDER SENTENCE OF DEATH FOR TREASON AND MURDER, AT CHARLESTOWN, VA.—FROM A PHOTOGRAPH TAKEN ONE YEAR AGO BY MARTIN M. LAWRENCE, 381 BROADWAY, N. Y.

Upon another occasion, a bo— of some two hundred and twen— men were raised and equipped — Jackson County, Mo., and sta— ed into Kansas under the comma— of General Whitfield, to atta— and capture "Old Brown," — every one called him. Brow— who was always vigilant a— wary, and was possessed of secr— means of intelligence, had ma— full preparation to meet the M— sourians, and was encamped w— one hundred and sixty men a— chosen point near the Santa — road, which he knew his enem— would pass. He had fifty men w— Sharpe's rifles, which would kill— half a mile, and which could — loaded at the breech and fir— with great rapidity, whom he h— had concealed in a ravine, lyi— on the ground, and commandi— the prairie for a mile before the— The residue of the party he h— concealed in the timber, ready — the proper moment for an atta— on the flank of those who mig— reach the ravine alive. Color— Sumner, with a squad of dragoo— came down from Fort Leaven —o— and prevented the fight, disbar— ing both parties, after which t— Colonel was heard to remark th— his interposition was a fortuna— event for the Missourians, as t— arrangements and preparatio— made by Brown would have — sured their destruction.

With respect to the ultima— fate of this man, there can be — question that his sentence will — carried out to the letter. T— Washington *States* says:

"We understand that Honoral— Fernando Wood, of New York, h— written to Governor Wise, of V— ginia, to know if the Governor — tends to pardon or commute t— sentence of old Brown. The Go— ernor has replied to Mr. Ex-May— Wood that old Ossawattami— Brown will certainly be hung — the 2nd day of December nex— when his body will be handed ov— to the surgeons to be taken fr— from the State, so that the carca— shall not pollute the soil of Vi— ginia."

The other conspirators ha— been sentenced to be hanged — the 10th of December—this wi— dispose of all of these wretche— men except Stephens, who ha— been handed over to the Feder— authorities for trial. This is don— for the purpose of subpœnai— some of the chief Abolitionists — we rather fancy, however, tha— there will be considerable difficul— in getting Greeley, Seward, Gi— dings and their compatriots o— the witness stand.

As a proof of the diseased sy— pathy felt for this man, we notic— that Governor Wise has had sever— letters from ladies requesting pe—

5 A NATION DIVIDED

ﾟᏟᎶᎬᏎᎭ

In 1859, Jackson got his first taste of the bloodshed that would rip the United States in two. In October, abolitionist John Brown seized a U.S. weapons storehouse in the small town of Harpers Ferry in what is now West Virginia. Brown wanted to start a rebellion of slaves in the South. The effort failed, and Brown was captured and sentenced to hang. John Brown became a hero for the antislavery movement.

Jackson and 21 of his military cadets were ordered to travel to Charlestown, Virginia (now West Virginia). Officials had received reports that Brown's supporters might try to rescue him. To prevent this from happening, Jackson and his men were stationed around the gallows. Jackson later described Brown's execution in a letter to his wife, Anna:

A newspaper article profiling John Brown's attempted rebellion

Brown had his arms tied behind him, and ascended the scaffold with apparent cheerfulness. After reaching the top of the platform, he shook hands with several who were standing around him. The sheriff placed the rope around his neck, then threw a white cap over his head, and asked him if he wished a signal when all should be ready. He replied that it made no difference, provided he was not kept waiting too long. ... I was much impressed with the thought that before me stood a man in the full vigor of health, who must in a few moments be in eternity. I sent up a petition that he might be saved. Awful was the thought that he might in a few minutes receive the sentence, "Depart, ye wicked, into everlasting fire!" I hope that he was prepared to die, but I am doubtful—he wouldn't have a minister with him.

In 1860, problems between the North and the South reached a boiling point. Southern states felt that Abraham Lincoln's victory in the presidential election threatened their place in the United States. In December, South Carolina seceded and was followed by Mississippi, Florida, Alabama, Georgia, Louisiana, and Texas. Two months later, these states formed the Confederate States of America. Four more states—Virginia, Arkansas, North Carolina, and Tennessee—would later join the Confederacy.

Jackson was not opposed to slavery. He owned

two slaves, and his wife owned four. He felt that the South and North should remain together. Anna later wrote, "Major Jackson was strongly for the Union, but at the same time he was a firm States'-rights man. ... He was never a secessionist, and maintained that it was better for the South to fight for her rights in the Union than out of it."

Nearly one-third of all Southern families owned slaves.

Still, Jackson chose to remain loyal to his home state when Virginia seceded on April 17, 1861. He offered to help Virginia in any way he could. On April 21, he was ordered to bring his cadets from

VMI to Richmond, Virginia. He left Lexington the same day. In Richmond, Jackson was made a colonel in Virginia's army. His first assignment was to train the Virginia men who had volunteered to fight for the Confederacy. His cadets served as drillmasters and helped him instruct the volunteers.

Jackson's success with his inexperienced volunteers earned him a promotion and some well-deserved respect. He demanded obedience from his men without argument or discussion. The sternness that had once made his students dislike him now earned him the trust and admiration of his soldiers. A former VMI cadet, now an officer serving under Jackson, wrote:

Jackson's 1st Brigade was made up of Virginians from the Shenandoah Valley and Virginia's western mountain area. These men were from all walks of life. Farmers, blacksmiths, carpenters, clerks, and "gentlemen" all fought with Jackson. There were even some students from theology school who named their cannons Matthew, Mark, Luke, and John, after the authors of the four gospels.

> *Jackson was much more in his element here as an army officer than when in the professor's chair at Lexington. It seemed that the sights and sounds of war had aroused his energies. His manner had become more forceful; his face was bronzed from exposure; his beard ... was unshorn.*

Jackson traveled to Richmond in 1861 to train volunteers to fight for the Confederacy.

Jackson's first battle command was at Harpers Ferry, where he had been two years earlier for John Brown's execution. Since that time, the town had become a symbol of the fight to end slavery. In addition, Harpers Ferry was important to both Union and Confederate armies. Many rifles used in the Civil War were made there. During the war, the town would serve as a supply base for the Union Army.

Jackson was ordered to hold the area for the South for as long as possible. Part of his charge was to bring discipline to the soldiers guarding the town. As a result, one of his first acts was to have all barrels of liquor destroyed.

Many said that Jackson and Little Sorrel were like kindred spirits. The horse's cremated remains are buried at VMI.

While at Harpers Ferry, Jackson bought his favorite horse. Although he purchased the animal for his wife, Jackson liked him so much that he decided to keep him for himself. The horse was originally named Fancy, but he was soon renamed Little

Sorrel. The animal was much like Jackson himself—tireless. Little Sorrel could travel up to 40 miles (64 km) per day, and his gait was so comfortable that Jackson sometimes fell asleep in the saddle. At the height of Jackson's fame, Southern ladies cut hairs from the horse's mane and tail to weave into bracelets. Today, Little Sorrel's cremated bones are buried at VMI, where his stuffed hide was displayed for years.

> *The town of Winchester changed hands more than 70 times during the Civil War. Nearly 8,000 men who died during local battles are buried in or near the town.*

In June 1861, Jackson was ordered to evacuate his men from Harpers Ferry and move to Winchester, Virginia. Before they left, Jackson's soldiers destroyed everything they couldn't take with them. Two bridges spanning the Shenandoah River were blown up, and shops and other buildings were burned. The Southern Army wanted to leave nothing behind that Union soldiers might be able to use. ℘

6 DEFENDING VIRGINIA

❧❦❧

In July 1861, the Union Army began invading Virginia. Jackson, now promoted to brigadier general, joined General P.G.T. Beauregard and his men at Manassas Junction. Located on Bull Run Creek, Manassas Junction was the site of an important railway station. From here, food and supplies were transported between northern and southern Virginia.

The first major battle of the Civil War began on July 21, when about 37,000 Union soldiers under the command of General Irwin McDowell attacked a force of 35,000 Confederate troops at Manassas Junction. The Union called the conflict the First Battle of Bull Run. In the South, the battle was called the Battle of First Manassas.

Civil War battles often had two names. The North chose names based on nearby bodies of water, while the South used the actual locations. This photo shows the ruins of a bridge at the site of the First Battle of Bull Run, or First Manassas.

Initially, the battle went poorly for the Confederacy. As Jackson and his men arrived at the scene of battle, wounded Confederate soldiers made their way past them, looking for aid. A Virginia soldier later described the sight:

General P.G.T. Beauregard

The wounded commenced passing us, some with the blood streaming down their faces, some with legs broken and hobbling along assisted by a comrade, and some seriously wounded and borne on stretchers. Those who could talk told us that their commands were cut all to pieces and the day was lost. Such talk ... was calculated to make a boy wish himself a thousand miles away and in the trundle bed at his mother's house.

Already, victory telegrams were being sent back to Union officials in Washington, D.C. The spectators who had traveled from the Union capital cheered as they watched the battle they hoped would bring an end to the Confederacy.

An exhausted General Barnard Bee, commander of South Carolina's troops, galloped up to Jackson. He said, "General, they are driving us." Jackson looked calmly at Bee and said, "Sir, we will give them the bayonet."

Jackson's soldiers continued to fire on the approaching Union troops. He walked among his men, speaking quietly, saying, "Steady, men, steady! All's well!" His presence encouraged retreating Confederate soldiers to turn around and hold firm. Before long, Jackson and his 1st Brigade captured the Union's artillery and aimed it at the enemy. "We have whipped them," Jackson cried. "They ran like dogs! Give me ten thousand men and I will take Washington tomorrow!"

The First Battle of Bull Run was a victory for the South. At the end of the day, 3,000 Union soldiers and 2,000 Confederate troops lay dead. Jackson himself was wounded, shot in the middle finger during the fighting. Although the finger was fractured, the wound would eventually heal.

The bravery and determination of the 1st Brigade brought fame to the men, as well as their commander.

During the First Battle of Bull Run, Jackson told his men to "yell like furies." In Greek mythology, furies were spirits who tormented criminals and other wrongdoers. Bull Run was the first time the famous rebel yell was heard on the battlefield. A soldier later described the call as follows: "The Rebels cheer like a lot of school boys, every man for himself."

From that day on, Jackson would be known simply as "Stonewall." His men were called the "Stonewall Brigade." Although the group was often dirty and disheveled, they were devoted to their general and fought hard. They called him "Old Jack," a nickname filled with respect and affection.

One of Jackson's men wrote a poem about him, which includes the lines:

> *We see him now—the old slouched hat,*
> *Cocked o'er his eye askew;*
> *The shrewd dry smile, the speech so pat,*
> *So calm, so blunt, so true.*
> *The 'Blue-light Elder' knows them well:*
> *Says he, 'That's Banks—he's fond of shell;*
> *Lord save his soul! we'll give him—' well,*
> *That's Stonewall Jackson's way.*

For the soldiers who came to love and admire him, Jackson's strange ways simply added to his growing legend. The men discussed his habit of napping for five minutes at a time. They noted that he frequently sucked on lemons and other citrus fruits. At the start of each battle, his face contorted with spasms. His men would say, "Old Jack is making faces at the Yankees."

After his finger was fractured, Jackson adopted another unusual habit. The wound had become infected after the battle, and to ease the pain Jackson raised his left hand so that the finger pointed

Although Jackson was popular with Southern troops, he was also renowned for odd habits and sometimes strange behavior.

upward. He continued to do this even after his finger healed. Because of his religious nature, many soldiers thought that Jackson was calling upon God to help him achieve victory.

Jackson's manner of dressing was another topic of discussion. Unlike other officers, he did not worry about wearing an old, wrinkled uniform or one that was dusty from marches or battle. Early in the war, he donned the plain blue uniform of VMI. More than a year after the war began, Confederate troops joked that the general had yet to change his shirt. One biographer wrote that Jackson looked "more scarecrow than human." And a fellow officer from North Carolina exclaimed: "What a common, ordinary looking man he is! There's nothing at all striking in his appearance."

Jackson's enemies were equally surprised by how he looked. After hearing tales of the legendary Stonewall, they expected to see a man of dignity and stature. An injured Northerner, captured by Jackson's men, asked to be lifted up to catch a glimpse of the general. A soldier from Alabama recalled what happened next:

The Civil War brought personal pain and heartache to Stonewall Jackson. As in other families, it split apart even the closest relatives. During the war, Union troops occupied his sister Laura's hometown of Beverly, Virginia. Laura cared for wounded Union soldiers under her roof. Because of her actions, she and Stonewall Jackson never spoke or wrote to each other again. She died in 1911, never having expressed any sorrow at choosing the Union over her beloved brother.

> *He surveyed the great Confederate general in his dingy gray uniform, with his cap pulled down on his brow, for half a minute, and then in a tone of disappointment and disgust exclaimed, "O my god! Lay me down!"*

Although General Jackson was admired by his own men, he was not well liked by some of the officers who served under him. Jackson refused to engage in polite conversations with his fellow officers.

General A.P. Hill called him "that crazy old Presbyterian fool." Another general, Richard Ewell, called him "that enthusiastic fanatic." Ewell and at least two other officers requested a transfer, while others resigned rather than serve under him.

Despite losing a leg in 1862, General Richard Ewell returned to active duty.

Jackson took his religion with him onto the battlefield. The night before a battle, he often prayed several times. When asked once about how he managed to remain brave in the face of enemy fire, he said, "God has fixed the time for my death. I do not concern myself about that, but to always be ready, no matter when it may overtake me." He added, "That is the way all men should live, then all would be equally brave."

7 THE SHENANDOAH VALLEY CAMPAIGN

ॐ

After the First Battle of Bull Run in 1861, Jackson was promoted to the rank of major general and assigned to defend the Shenandoah Valley. The Shenandoah River region of Virginia was home to some of the richest farmland in the country. The area was a major food supplier to the Confederate Army. For this reason, it was called the Breadbasket of the Confederacy.

Because of its importance to the South, the Shenandoah Valley became a target for the North. The Union Army wanted to take control of the area and cut off the South's source of food. Jackson understood that this must be prevented at all costs. He said, "If this Valley is lost, Virginia is lost."

In 1861, Jackson prepared to defend the Shenandoah Valley.

Jackson was called on to defend the valley, but his famous Stonewall Brigade had been ordered to stay behind. Parting from the soldiers who had fought so hard for him was an emotional moment. Jackson rode out to the field on Little Sorrel and spoke to his men for what he feared would be the last time.

> *You have endured hard marches ... exposure and privations ... like men and patriots. You are the brigade which turned the tide of battle on Manassas Plains and there gained for yourself imperishable honor, and your names will be handed down with honor attached in future history. You were the First Brigade in the Army of the Shenandoah, the First Brigade in the Army of the Potomac ... and are the First Brigade in the hearts of your generals. ... In the future ... I expect to hear of crowning deeds of valor and of victories gloriously achieved! May God bless you all! Farewell!*

By the end of the speech, many of Jackson's men were weeping. After a moment of silence, they began to cheer. This was the beginning of a tradition: Southern troops would cheer whenever Stonewall and his staff rode by.

Not much happened during Jackson's first winter in the Shenandoah Valley. The only action

Jackson and his men saw was an expedition to take Romney, a small but important village in present-day West Virginia. At this time, the little town was

Southern troops rallied and cheered whenever Jackson rode by.

occupied by Union troops. On New Year's Day, in 1862, Jackson's army set out for Romney. The weather was mild, and the spirits of the soldiers were high.

Just hours later, the mood quickly changed. The temperature dropped, and men who had left their overcoats on the supply wagons began to shiver. By the end of the day, the cold wind blew so strongly that it was impossible to light a campfire. Soldiers huddled together on the frozen ground for warmth. Those who had left their blankets behind were especially uncomfortable.

For the rest of the march, the men would brave icy winds, freezing temperatures, and steady snowfall. The supply wagons with food for the soldiers were unable to keep up, and the men were hungry. As they trudged through the snow, the soldiers—and some of the officers—began to grumble.

One soldier from Tennessee remembered, "They called him 'Tom Fool Jackson.' They blamed him for the cold weather; they blamed him for everything." Although the officers were angry, too, they continued to follow Jackson's orders.

During the expedition, Jackson's men captured the town of Bath before moving on toward their goal: Romney. The march from one town to the other was brutal. A Virginia soldier described the scene:

The road was almost an uninterrupted sheet of ice, rendering it almost impossible for man or beast to travel, while by moonlight the beards of the men (not mine), matted with ice & glistening with crystals presented a very peculiar yet ludicrous appearance.

In 1862, Jackson's troops endured a brutal march from Bath to Romney.

When the men finally reached Romney, they found that the Union troops had abandoned the town. On January 14, Stonewall Jackson entered and took control of Romney.

Nine days later, Jackson left General William Loring and his men in charge of Romney and headed back for Winchester. Although Jackson may have thought he was doing Loring a favor by allowing his troops to rest, the general was furious with his new command. In the words of one soldier, Romney was a "miserable hole" and a "hog pen." Loring appealed to the Confederate secretary of war, Judah Philip Benjamin, who ordered Jackson to allow the general and his men to return to Winchester.

Jackson did as he was commanded but then promptly resigned. No one, he felt, should second-guess his orders. One of Stonewall's officers described the reaction to the resignation:

> *The army became excited, the people of the Valley indignant. Jackson was cool and immovable. The governor of Virginia interposed, and the Secretary of War yielded. Loring was sent elsewhere, and Jackson resumed his command, and this was the last time the War Department ever undertook to interfere with his proper authority.*

Despite the turmoil of the Romney Expedition, some of Jackson's happiest moments during the war came that winter when his wife visited Winchester. Anna arrived in mid-January. Together, the couple celebrated Jackson's 38th birthday. Anna remained with her husband until early March, when he felt that Winchester was no longer safe. He was right. Soon after Anna returned home, the Union Army captured the town.

In the spring of 1862, the war in the valley heated up. As the cold, snowy weather faded away, Jackson began his famous Shenandoah Valley Campaign. His mission was to prevent reinforcements from reaching Union General George B. McClellan, who was headed to Richmond from the east. Jackson intended to do this by marching toward Washington, D.C., pretending that he was going to attack the Union capital. With any luck, troops that had been sent to help McClellan would be sent back to defend the capital city.

Jackson had several advantages over Northern troops in the Shenandoah Valley.

With his military skills and knowledge of the Shenandoah Valley, Jackson had an advantage over the Union generals he would soon face. The Northerners were new to warfare and the area. In addition, Jackson's victory at Manassas had boosted the confidence of Southern troops everywhere. In the North, Jackson had an opposite effect. Tales of

In November 1861, Stonewall and his fierce, fearless fighting style
General George struck terror into the Union troops.
B. McClellan
was appointed   Jackson began his campaign on March 23, 1862,
commander-in-chief
of the Union Army. by attacking Union troops under the command of

James Shields at Kernstown, near Winchester. Even though it was Sunday, Jackson put aside his religious convictions to battle the enemy. Fighting alongside him was the Stonewall Brigade. The new Confederate secretary of war, George Wythe Randolph, had ordered Jackson's old troops to follow him.

At the Battle of Kernstown, Jackson and about 3,000 men attacked a force of Union troops more than twice their size. The battle raged until nightfall, when Confederate troops fled into the darkness. Shields was the only Northern general who would be able to say he had defeated Stonewall Jackson. Yet the battle was still a tactical success for the Confederate commander. Jackson had prevented Northern troops from advancing any farther toward Richmond.

> *The Battle of Kernstown was the first major battle in Jackson's Shenandoah Valley Campaign. It was also the general's only major defeat (though a tactical success). Before the conflict, Jackson broke one of his own rules of battle. Instead of assessing the enemy's position for himself, he relied solely on information from one of his officers. The faulty information cost the South the battle.*

In April, Jackson headed into the mountains of western Virginia. He and his men attacked one Union force after another, surprising them and pushing them back toward Washington. The general's troops became known for their "lightning marches."

Most battles of the Civil War were fought in the South.

On some marches, the soldiers covered more than 40 miles (64 km) in one day. Jackson's men moved so quickly that they became known as "foot cavalry."

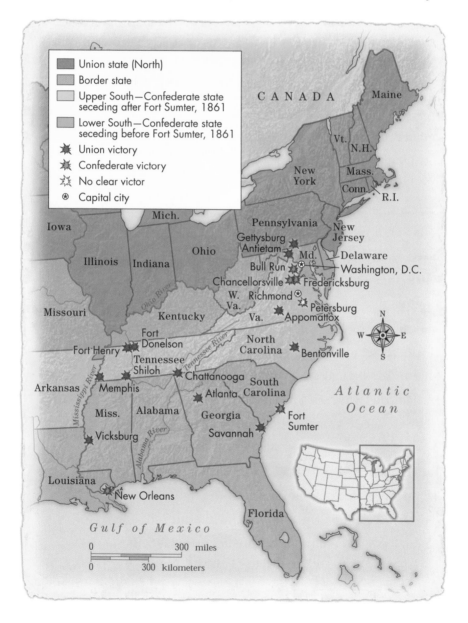

Union state (North)
Border state
Upper South—Confederate state seceding after Fort Sumter, 1861
Lower South—Confederate state seceding before Fort Sumter, 1861
Union victory
Confederate victory
No clear victor
Capital city

CANADA

Maine

Vt.
N.H.
New York
Mass.
Conn.
R.I.

Mich.
Iowa
Pennsylvania
New Jersey
Gettysburg
Antietam
Ohio
Md.
Delaware
Illinois
Indiana
Bull Run
Washington, D.C.
Chancellorsville
Fredericksburg
W. Va.
Richmond
Missouri
Kentucky
Va.
Petersburg
Appomattox
Fort Donelson
North Carolina
Bentonville
Fort Henry
Tennessee
Shiloh
Chattanooga
South Carolina
Arkansas
Memphis
Atlanta
Miss.
Alabama
Georgia
Fort Sumter
Vicksburg
Savannah

Ohio River
Tennessee River
Mississippi River
Alabama River

Atlantic Ocean

N
W   E
S

Louisiana
New Orleans

Florida

Gulf of Mexico

0   300 miles
0   300 kilometers

Many war historians believe that Jackson's 1862 Shenandoah Valley Campaign was one of the most brilliant tactical campaigns ever waged. Although the number of men he commanded varied from 3,000 to 32,000, Jackson was able to drive out forces up to three times larger than his own. One of his favorite techniques was known as a flanking maneuver. He ordered some of his troops to move around the enemy and surprise them from behind.

Just as he had used willpower and hard work to pull up his grades at West Point, he did the same to succeed in the valley. While talking to General John D. Imboden, Jackson explained his theories on warfare and battle tactics:

> *There are two things never to be lost sight of by a military commander. Always mystify, mislead, and surprise the enemy, if possible. And when you strike and overcome him, never give up the pursuit as long as your men have the strength to follow. ... The other rule is, never fight against heavy odds, if by a possible maneuvering you can hurl your own force on only a part ... of your enemy and crush it. Such tactics will win every time, and a small army may thus destroy a large one.*

On May 8, Jackson and his men defeated the troops of General John C. Frémont at the village

Union General John C. Frémont was famous long before the Civil War. Known throughout the country as the "Pathfinder," Frémont explored the area between the Rocky Mountains and the Pacific Ocean during the 1840s. He used his experiences to create the first scientific map of the western United States. In 1856, Frémont was the first Republican candidate for president. He was defeated by James Buchanan. Frémont survived the war and served as Arizona's first territorial governor from 1878 to 1883.

of McDowell, in Virginia. Two weeks later, Jackson began an assault in the valley that would bring his campaign there to an end. On May 23, Jackson and his men attacked the troops of General Nathaniel P. Banks at Front Royal, Virginia. The battle lasted two days and ended with Banks and his men fleeing Winchester and heading back across the Potomac River.

After Jackson's victory at Winchester, Union troops in the area were ordered to return to Washington. Union officials expected that Jackson's next move would be to cross the Potomac River and attack the capital. They wanted soldiers there to defend the city.

Jackson's plan had worked. He had tied up the Union soldiers in the Shenandoah Valley and prevented them from marching to Richmond. Without the needed reinforcements, McClellan's troops outside of Richmond would now be more vulnerable to Robert E. Lee's army. Jackson headed south,

defeating Union troops sent to chase after him and his men. By sheer inventiveness, Jackson won several victories in the Shenandoah Valley, including battles at Cross Keys and Port Republic, Virginia. ❧

The Battle of Cross Keys was a victory for the South on June 8, 1862.

Chapter

8 LEE'S RIGHT-HAND MAN

_{coros}

Jackson's victories in the Shenandoah Valley made him famous throughout the country and around the world. He became known for defeating enemy forces that outnumbered his own. During his campaign to defend the Shenandoah Valley, he fought in six battles and initiated a dozen actions that delayed Union troops. About 7,000 Northern soldiers died; Southern troops suffered only about half those losses. Jackson's soldiers also seized weapons and supplies from the retreating Northern Army. Jackson's final report on the campaign ended: "God has been our shield, and to His name be all the glory."

In the South, Stonewall Jackson was a hero. At a time when there was little good news for the Confederacy, he provided hope and inspiration to

As the Civil War progressed, Jackson's fame as a commander grew.

Southerners. In June 1862, a Georgia newspaper showed the public's growing fondness for Jackson:

> *Sometime ago, we accused Jackson of being of unsound mind. Since that time he has exhibited not the least symptom of improvement. In fact he gets worse and worse every day. Within the last two weeks he seems to have gone clean daft ... He has been raving, ramping, roaring, rearing, snorting and cavorting up and down the Valley, chawing up Yankees by the thousands. ... Crazy or not, we but echo the voice of the whole Confederacy when we say "God bless Old Stonewall."*

While he was viewed as a hero in his own land, Jackson was seen as a terror by Northern troops. One Southern soldier called him the "great dread of the Yankees." Another said that Jackson's mere presence was enough to "strike fear into the heart of the enemy."

Another Southern hero was General Robert E. Lee, commander-in-chief of the Confederate Army. Like Jackson, he chose to remain loyal to Virginia, despite being offered command of all the Union forces. By now, he realized that Stonewall Jackson was his most brilliant commander. After hearing of his success in the Shenandoah Valley, Lee ordered Jackson to help fight off McClellan's troops in Richmond.

Jackson and his men began one of their lightning marches. But Jackson was in unfamiliar territory. While General Lee and his troops were being beaten by McClellan's men at Mechanicsville, a town north of Richmond, Stonewall was still busy trying to reach him. Union soldiers had chopped down trees and destroyed bridges to make the trip even more difficult. By the time Jackson's men arrived on June 27, they were exhausted. Jackson may have also been suffering from stress.

General Robert E. Lee, commander of the Confederate Army

Jackson's performance at this battle and the other battles that made up the "Seven Days' Battles" was not impressive. But he managed to capture a dozen Union troops. When the prisoners were brought behind Confederate lines, one boasted, "Gentlemen, we had the honor of being captured by Stonewall Jackson himself." At the end of a week, the Southerners defeated McClellan, driving him from the Confederate capital.

Together, Lee and Jackson seemed unstoppable, and modern historians still refer to their relationship as one of the best military partnerships of all time.

Jackson said, "So great is my confidence in General Lee that I am willing to follow him blindfolded." Lee came to regard Jackson as his top commander.

After defeating Union troops in Culpepper County, Virginia, Jackson moved on to join Lee at Manassas Junction. There the Union Army waited. Although Northern troops had been defeated in Richmond, the soldiers now had a new commander, General John Pope. He had made camp near

General John Pope

Bull Run Creek and prepared to launch a second attack on the Confederate capital.

To prevent the attack, Lee sent Jackson orders to attack Pope's troops from the rear. On August 28, the fighting began. A Confederate soldier later told of his own experience at the Second Battle of Bull Run:

The battle, now more furious than before, swayed to and fro; and for sometime doubtful conclusions hung in the balance. ... The contest constantly grew fiercer and more bloody. Often the combatants delivered their fire against each other within ten or a dozen paces. ... The slaughter was too horrible and sickening.

The Second Battle of Bull Run

At the end of the battle, Southern troops sent Pope's men into a hasty retreat. Nearly 14,000 Union soldiers and 8,000 Confederate soldiers were killed or wounded. Jackson and his men pursued the fleeing soldiers and drove them back to Washington.

Now the Confederate Army moved north, intent on attacking Maryland. In early September, Lee and his men crossed the Potomac. With his arrival in Maryland, Lee expected McClellan and

Jackson captured Harpers Ferry in September 1862.

his troops to leave Harpers Ferry and move north. When they didn't, Lee ordered Jackson to capture Harpers Ferry.

On September 10, Jackson and his 14,000 men left Frederick, Maryland, and headed toward their target. In two days, the men marched 51 miles (82 km). They moved through southern Maryland, crossing the Potomac and capturing Martinsburg, Virginia (now part of West Virginia). On September 13, Southern soldiers in Martinsburg began firing cannons and other weapons at Harpers Ferry.

A Union soldier at the battle wrote in his diary, "All seem to think that we will have to surrender or be cut to pieces." For two days, the town withstood the bombardment. Then on September 15, the Union troops at Harpers Ferry finally surrendered. More than 12,500 Union soldiers were taken prisoner, the highest number captured during the Civil War. Jackson and his men also confiscated 13,000 weapons and 47 pieces of artillery.

Two days after his victory at Harpers Ferry, Jackson led his troops back across the Potomac to Sharpsburg, Maryland. Here General Lee's divided forces were being attacked by Northern troops under McClellan's command. Jackson arrived in time to prevent Lee's forces from being destroyed. In the North, the conflict became known as the Battle of Antietam because it was fought near Antietam Creek. In the South, the battle became known as the Battle of Sharpsburg.

The conflict was the most deadly battle of the entire war: 13,000 Union soldiers were dead or missing. Lee lost 10,000 soldiers and was forced out of Maryland and back into Virginia. One of Jackson's doctors described the bloody battle scene:

[The old Stonewall Division] had been reduced to a very small body of men and were commanded by Col. Grigsby ... While talking to Grigsby, I saw off at a distance in a field men lying down, and supposed it was a line of battle.

I asked Colonel Grigsby why he did not move that line of battle to make it conform to his own, when he said, "Those men ... are all dead ... They are Georgia soldiers."

The Battle of Antietam on September 17, 1862, was the single bloodiest day in Civil War history. More than 23,000 men were wounded or killed. The battle prompted President Abraham Lincoln to issue the Emancipation Proclamation, which declared all Southern slaves free. Although Lincoln had written the proclamation months before the battle, the violence and horror of Antietam strengthened his resolve to end the war as quickly as possible. The president hoped that freeing the slaves in rebellious states would weaken the Confederate Army by forcing Southerners to stay at home and tend to their homes and farms.

Back on Southern soil, Lee now divided his army into two groups. One group, the 1st Corps, was under the command of General James Longstreet.

The 2nd Corps was under the command of Jackson, now promoted to the rank of lieutenant general. Lee himself had recommended Stonewall for his new title. He wrote that Jackson was "true, honest, and brave; has a single eye to the good of the service and spares no exertion to accomplish his objective."

For the next two months, both the Confederate and Union armies rested. This gave Lee the chance to reorganize and have fresh supplies brought up to the battle lines. In Washington, President Lincoln had become impatient with McClellan's failure to pursue Lee after the Battle of Antietam. Lincoln fired his top commander, replacing him with General Ambrose E. Burnside. In the second week of December 1862, Burnside advanced to Fredericksburg, Virginia, to attack the Confederate

The Battle of Antietam marks one of the bloodiest days in American history.

81

Army camped there. Afterward, he expected to march on Richmond.

On December 11, the Battle of Fredericksburg began. Burnside commanded about 120,000 troops, while Lee had less than 80,000. General Longstreet described the difference in the two armies' appearances:

Before the Battle of Fredericksburg, Jackson received some good news from home. He was a father! He asked his wife to name the baby girl Julia, after his mother. He worried about losing the small child, as he had lost his first two. "Do not set your affections upon her, except as a gift of God. If she absorbs too much of our hearts, God may remove her from us."

The flags of the Federals fluttered gaily, the polished arms shone brightly in the sunlight, and the beautiful uniforms of the ... troops gave to the scene the air of a holiday occasion. ...

I could almost see every soldier [the Union commander] had, and a splendid array it was. ... Jackson's ragged infantry and ... Stuart's battered cavalry ... [were] a striking contrast to the handsomely equipped troops of the Federals.

The Confederates may not have been much to look at, but they were a force to be reckoned with. For hours, Union troops tried to defeat the Southern Army. In the end, however, Lee and Jackson crushed Burnside and his men.

The Battle of Fredericksburg was the most

decisive Confederate victory of the war. At the end of the day, more than 12,500 Union soldiers had been killed or wounded. The South lost 5,000 troops. As a result of the defeat, General Burnside was relieved of command of the Union Army.

The battle ignited the need for retaliation by Union forces at Gettysburg. It also added to Jackson's reputation as a brilliant military commander. To many, he seemed unbeatable, and his legend continued to grow. ✺

Jackson's daughter Julia was named after his mother.

9 CHANCELLORSVILLE AND TRAGEDY

❧❧❧❧

After Fredericksburg, the Union and Confederate armies spent the winter of 1862–1863 camped near Fredericksburg, on either side of the Rappahanock River in Virginia. Throughout the winter, both armies were content to sit and wait until warmer weather allowed the fighting to resume.

During this time, Jackson wrote official reports on their battles. He also drilled his men, getting them ready for the fight to come. Finally, in April 1863, Lee and Jackson moved their men to Chancellorsville, Virginia.

Late in the month, Jackson allowed his wife and infant daughter to visit. Afterward, Anna described the delight he took in his new baby:

The Battle of Chancellorsville was known as Robert E. Lee's greatest victory.

He rarely had her out of his arms, walking her, and amusing her in every way that he could think of—sometimes holding her up before a mirror and saying, admiringly, "Now, Miss Jackson, look at yourself!" Then he would turn ... and say: "Isn't she a little gem?"

When she slept ... he would kneel over her cradle and gaze upon her little face with the most rapt admiration, and he said he felt almost as if she were an angel, in her innocence and purity.

But even as Jackson got to know his new baby, he learned that Yankee soldiers were drawing near. After nine days together, the family had to part.

At Chancellorsville, the Northern soldiers were led by General Joseph Hooker. He had replaced Burnside after the disastrous battle at Fredericksburg. Hooker's army outnumbered the Confederates by nearly two to one. Despite this fact, Jackson took 28,000 men and began preparing to attack the Union Army from the rear.

The battle started on May 1. On May 2, Jackson struck, surprising Hooker's men. The South won easily, and Hooker and his troops fled. The Battle of Chancellorsville became known as Lee's greatest victory, and his success was due in large part to Jackson. Lee later wrote in his official report of the battle that "the fortune of the day decided was con-

ducted by ... Lieutenant-General Jackson." He called
what would be Jackson's last command "a worthy
conclusion of that long series of splendid achieve-
ments which won for him the lasting love and grati-
tude of his country."

A tragic accident after the battle brought
Jackson's brilliant career to an abrupt end. That
evening, he rode out to the front lines to watch
Hooker and his troops flee. But as Jackson returned
to the Confederate line after dark, disaster struck.
Unable to identify the famous fighter, Confederate

*General Joseph
Hooker at
Chancellorsville*

Jackson was accidentally shot three times by his own men. Two of the wounds were minor, but the one in his arm was serious.

troops opened fire on Jackson and his party. In the fading light, the men had mistaken Jackson for a Yankee spy. The general's aid, James Smith, later recorded the event:

The left company began firing ... and two of his party fell from their saddles dead. ...

Spurring his horse across the road to his right, he was met by a second volley. ... Under this volley ... the general received three balls at the same instant. ...

His horse turned quickly from the fire, through the thick bushes, which swept the cap from the general's head and scratched his forehead, leaving drops of blood to stain his face. As he lost his hold upon the bridle-rein, he reeled from the saddle and was caught ... [and] laid upon the ground.

Two of Jackson's wounds were minor. One bullet passed through Jackson's left forearm and the other lodged in the palm of his right hand. But the third bullet hit Jackson in the left arm below the shoulder and seriously wounded him. He was placed on a litter, and four soldiers carried him to the medical tent at the back of the battle lines. On the way, one of the men was struck by a Union shell and dropped his end of the litter. Jackson fell about 5 feet (1.5 m) to the ground and injured his arm even more.

After examining Jackson's wounds, battlefield physicians believed that he would recover if his left arm was amputated. Jackson agreed to the surgery. He was given medicine to ease the pain and make him unconscious during the operation. His arm was amputated about 2 inches (5 centimeters) below his shoulder. The surgeon also took the bullet out of Jackson's right palm. The surgery was a success.

When news of Jackson's surgery reached Lee, he couldn't hold back his tears. He said, "He has lost his left arm; but I have lost my right arm." General Lee then ordered that his top commander be immediately moved to Guiney Station, Virginia, which was behind the lines and out of harm's way. Jackson was placed in a horse-drawn wagon and suffered a bumpy 27-mile (43-km) ride to the railway station. Along the way, men and women rushed to the makeshift ambulance, offering

Jackson's fellow officers were devastated by the seriousness of his condition.

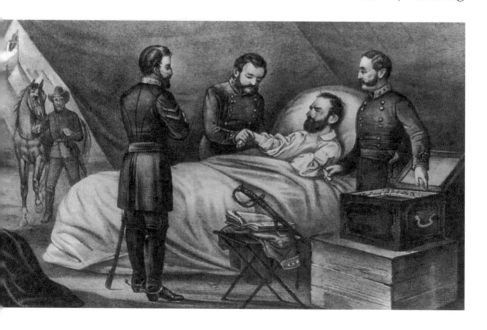

words of support, prayers, and food. At Guiney Station, Jackson was taken to the nearby Chandler House. Ever the gentleman, Jackson apologized to his host for not being able to shake his hand.

At first, Jackson seemed to be recovering well. The fifth day after surgery, however, he caught pneumonia, and his condition suddenly worsened. Jackson's wife and daughter hurried to his side. As Anna sang hymns to him, her husband drifted in and out of consciousness. Sometimes he shouted out battle orders to officers who weren't there. At other times, he was alert and spoke words of comfort to his wife.

On Saturday, May 9, Jackson was told he was dying. He said, "I see from the number of physicians that you think my condition dangerous, but I thank God, if it is His will, that I am ready to go."

The next day, Jackson awoke and said, "Let us cross over the river and rest under the trees." Then he died. Thomas "Stonewall" Jackson was 39 years old.

Upon learning of Jackson's death, Robert E. Lee declared, "I know not how to replace him." Southern soldiers saw Jackson's death as a bad omen. A former student noted that his passing

Upon hearing the news of Jackson's surgery, Lee sent a letter to him that said, "Could I have directed events, I should have chosen for the good of the country to have been disabled in your stead."

During the Civil War, most amputated limbs were buried in mass graves. But Jackson's arm was placed in the family cemetery of one of his chaplains. The grave remained unmarked until 1903. At that time, one of Jackson's former aides put a granite marker over it. Jackson's arm is currently buried in Ellwood Cemetery in Spotsylvania, Virginia. The rest of his body is buried in Lexington.

was "a national calamity," and a Confederate soldier from Alabama wrote, "I think the North will whip us soon." Even Confederate President Jefferson Davis, who did not value Jackson when he was alive, was devastated. After Jackson's funeral, a friend found the president staring off into space. He apologized, saying, "You must forgive me. I am still staggering from a dreadful blow. I cannot think."

Even Jackson's Union enemies acknowledged his greatness. General Gouverneur K. Warren wrote that the Union would be better off with Stonewall gone but added, "Yet in my soldier's heart I cannot but see him the best soldier of all this war, and grieve his untimely end."

Jackson's body was taken to Richmond, where it lay in state at the governor's mansion. His coffin was wrapped in a Confederate flag. Southerners were overcome with grief: Their hero, the man they had thought to be invincible, was dead. Twenty thousand people visited the mansion to pay their last respects to one of the greatest generals the nation had ever seen.

Jackson's gravesite in Lexington

As he had requested, Jackson was taken home to Lexington. Before he was buried, his body lay in state in his old classroom at VMI. After his burial, churches across the South held memorial services in his honor.

Jackson's widow made sure that no one would forget her husband and his sacrifice. She encouraged Robert Lewis Dabney, who had served in the military with Jackson, to write his biography. Anna never remarried, and she became known as the

A monument to Jackson, showing the commander with his beloved Little Sorrel.

THOMAS JONATHAN
JACKSON
1824   1863

"THERE STANDS JACKSON LIKE A STONEWALL"

"widow of the Confederacy." Later, she wrote her own book about her husband.

After the Confederacy was defeated, many Southerners maintained that the loss of Jackson was the turning point in the war. The Confederates believed that if Jackson had been alive to lead them, the South would have won. Even modern historians recognize Jackson's remarkable ability as a leader in battle.

Today, the memory of Thomas Jackson is alive and well in the South. Each year, Virginia recognizes Lee-Jackson Day, a state holiday that commemorates the birthdays of both Robert E. Lee and Jackson. Famous statues of Stonewall Jackson are scattered throughout the South. One statue, showing Jackson atop Little Sorrel, is at the Manassas National Battlefield in Virginia. There is also a Stonewall Jackson Shrine at the Fredericksburg and Spotsylvania National Military Park in Virginia.

Though he fought for the South, Jackson will be remembered by Americans everywhere for his amazing courage in battle and determination to succeed. Cherished by his troops and respected by his enemies, Stonewall Jackson's brilliant military career and role in the Civil War have made an indelible mark on U.S. history.

After his master's death, Little Sorrel lived with Anna Jackson in Lexington until 1883. When she could no longer care for him, he was sent to VMI. A doctor at the school recalled that whenever shots were fired by practicing cadets, the horse would "come running onto the parade ground, sniffing the air and snorting loudly, head and tail up, running up and down in front of the parade line." Another witness said that the animal pepped up when he heard the song "Dixie." Little Sorrel died in 1886, at the age of 36.

JACKSON'S LIFE

1846

Graduates from the
U.S. Military Academy
at West Point

1824

Born in
Clarksburg, Virginia

1825   1845

1826

The first photograph
is taken by
Joseph Niépce, a
French physicist

1846

German astronomer
Johann Gottfried
Galle discovers
Neptune

1836

Texans defeat
Mexican troops
at San Jacinto
after a deadly battle
at the Alamo

WORLD EVENTS

1851

Leaves the Army to teach at Virginia Military Institute

1853

Marries Elinor Junkin

1852

Postage stamps begin to be used widely

1850

Jeans are invented by Levi Strauss, a German who moved to California during the gold rush

JACKSON'S LIFE

1854

Elinor dies while
giving birth to
their son

1857

Marries Mary
Anna Morrison

1858

Daughter Mary
dies shortly
after her birth

1855

1856

Nikola Tesla,
electrical engineer
and inventor, is born

1858

English scientist
Charles Darwin
presents his theory
of evolution

WORLD EVENTS

1859

Guards abolitionist John Brown at his execution

1861

Virginia secedes from the Union in April; First Battle of Bull Run takes place in July and earns Jackson the nickname "Stonewall;" promoted to major general

1860

1860

Austrian composer Gustav Mahler is born in Kalischt (now in Austria)

1859

A Tale of Two Cities by Charles Dickens is published

JACKSON'S LIFE

1862

Begins Shenandoah
Valley campaign

1862

Victor Hugo publishes
Les Misérables

WORLD EVENTS

1863

Leads a surprise attack against General Joseph Hooker and his troops in the Battle of Chancellorsville; accidentally shot by his own troops and has his arm amputated; dies at age 39 on May 10

1863

Thomas Nast draws the modern Santa Claus for *Harper's Weekly*, although Santa existed previously

1865

The first fax is sent from Lyon to Paris, France

DATE OF BIRTH: January 21, 1824

BIRTHPLACE: Clarksburg, Virginia

FATHER: Jonathan (1790–1826)

MOTHER: Julia (1798–1831)

EDUCATION: U.S. Military Academy at West Point in New York

FIRST SPOUSE: Elinor Junkin (1825–1854)

DATE OF MARRIAGE: 1853

CHILDREN: Infant son died at birth (1854)

SECOND SPOUSE: Mary Anna Morrison (1831–1915)

DATE OF MARRIAGE: 1857

CHILDREN: Mary died shortly after birth (1858); Julia Laura (1862–1889)

DATE OF DEATH: May 10, 1863

PLACE OF BURIAL: Lexington, Virginia

IN THE LIBRARY

Brager, Bruce L. *There He Stands: The Story of Stonewall Jackson.* Greensboro, N.C.: Morgan Reynolds Publishing, 2004.

Editors of Time-Life Books. *Shenandoah, 1862.* Alexandria, Va.: Time-Life Books, 1997.

Harmon, Daniel E. *Civil War Generals.* Philadelphia: Chelsea House Publishers, 1997.

Moore, Kay, and Anni Matsick (illustrator). *If You Lived at the Time of the Civil War.* New York: Scholastic, 1994.

LOOK FOR MORE SIGNATURE LIVES BOOKS ABOUT THIS ERA:

Jefferson Davis: *President of the Confederate States of America*

Frederick Douglass: *Slave, Writer, Abolitionist*

William Lloyd Garrison: *Abolitionist and Journalist*

Ulysses S. Grant: *Union General and U.S. President*

Robert E. Lee: *Confederate Commander*

Abraham Lincoln: *Great American President*

Harriet Beecher Stowe: *Author and Advocate*

Elizabeth Van Lew: *Civil War Spy*

ON THE WEB

For more information on *Stonewall Jackson*, use FactHound to track down Web sites related to this book.

1. Go to *www.facthound.com*
2. Type in a search word related to this book or this book ID: 0756509874
3. Click on the *Fetch It* button.

FactHound will find the best Web sites for you.

HISTORIC SITES

Fredericksburg and Spotsylvania National Military Park
120 Chatham Lane
Fredericksburg, VA 22405-2508
540/373-4510
To visit a military park that stands where some of the bloodiest battles of the Civil War were waged

Stonewall Jackson Museum
33229 Old Valley Pike
Strasburg, VA
540/465-5884
To visit a museum that features information about the Civil War and the famous Confederate commander

abolitionists
people who worked to end slavery before the
Civil War

bayonet
a long knife fastened to the end of a rifle

cadets
young people who are training to become
members of the armed forces

company
an army unit under the command of a captain

Confederate
having to do with the Confederacy, or Southern
forces that broke away from the federal
government during the Civil War

litter
a stretcher used to transport someone who has
been wounded

maneuver
a movement by soldiers that is used as a military
strategy during battle

optics
the study of vision

regiment
a military unit made up of two or more battalions

tactical campaigns
plans of action that are used during battle

typhoid fever
a disease accompanied by fever, headache, and
severe intestinal problems

Union
Northern states that remained loyal to the federal
government during the Civil War

Chapter 1

Page 10, line 4: Mary Anna Jackson. *Life and Letters of "Stonewall" Jackson by His Wife.* New York: Harper and Brothers, 1892, p. 179.

Page 12, line 13: Ibid, p. 283.

Chapter 2

Page 16, line 5: James I. Robertson. *Stonewall Jackson: The Man, the Soldier, the Legend.* New York, Macmillan Publishing USA, 1997, p. 9.

Page 18, line 3: http://www.vmi.edu/archives/jackson/tj500706.html

Page 18, line 11: Richard Wheeler. *We Knew Stonewall Jackson.* New York: Thomas Y. Crowell Company, 1977, p. 5.

Page 20, line 6: Robert K. Krick. "Stonewall Jackson's deadly calm." *American Heritage,* Dec. 1996, v47, n8, p. 56.

Page 20, line 15: G.F.R. Henderson. *Stonewall Jackson and the American Civil War.* New York: Barnes & Noble Books, 1993, p. 15.

Page 20, line 27: *Life and Letters of "Stonewall" Jackson by His Wife,* p. 35.

Page 21, line 4: http://www.vmi.edu/archives/jackson/tj440908.html

Page 22, line 6: "Thomas Jackson." *DISCovering Biography.* Online Edition. Detroit: Gale, 2004.

Chapter 3

Page 25, line 14: Ibid.

Page 26, line 7: *We Knew Stonewall Jackson,* p. 7.

Page 28, line 1: http://www.vmi.edu/archives/jackson/tj480410.html

Page 29, sidebar: http://www.vmi.edu/archives/jackson/tj600416.html

Page 30, line 12: http://www.vmi.edu/archives/jackson/tj490427.html

Page 31, line 4: http://www.vmi.edu/archives/jackson/tj480905.html

Chapter 4

Page 35, sidebar: *Stonewall Jackson: The Man, the Soldier, the Legend,* p. 111.

Page 37, line 2: http://www.vmi.edu/archives/jackson/tjjprof.html

Page 38, line 13: Ibid, p. 137.

Page 38, line 21: "Stonewall Jackson's deadly calm."

Page 39, line 6: http://www.vmi.edu/archives/jackson/tj531019.html

Page 39, line 11: "Stonewall Jackson's deadly calm."

Page 40, line 9: *We Knew Stonewall Jackson,* p. 18.

Page 41, line 2: http://www.vmi.edu/archives/jackson/tj590219.html

Chapter 5

Page 44, line 1: *Life and Letters of "Stonewall" Jackson by His Wife,* pp. 130-131.

Page 45, line 3: *We Knew Stonewall Jackson,* p. 25.

Page 46, line 21: Ibid, p. 35.

Chapter 6

Page 53, sidebar: *Stonewall Jackson: The Man, the Soldier, the Legend,* p. 266.

Page 53, Ibid, p. 261.

Page 53, Ibid, p. 263.

Page 53, line 4: *Life and Letters of "Stonewall" Jackson by His Wife,* p. 178.

Page 53, line 12: *Stonewall Jackson: The Man, the Soldier, the Legend,* p. 269.

Page 53, line 18: *We Knew Stonewall Jackson,* p. 53.

Page 55, line 9: *Life and Letters of "Stonewall" Jackson by His Wife*, p. 286.

Page 54, line 23: *Stonewall Jackson: The Man, the Soldier, the Legend*, p. 342.

Page 56, line 6: "Thomas Jackson."

Page 56, line 7: "Stonewall Jackson's deadly calm."

Page 56, line 20: *We Knew Stonewall Jackson*, pp. 87-88.

Page 57, line 12: "Stonewall Jackson's deadly calm."

Page 57, line 15: Ibid.

Page 57, line 23: "Thomas Jackson."

Chapter 7

Page 59, line 14: James I. Robertson. "The Christian Soldier: General Thomas J. 'Stonewall' Jackson." *History Today*, Feb. 2003, v53, i2, p. 29.

Page 60, line 8: *Stonewall Jackson: The Man, the Soldier, the Legend*, pp. 282-283.

Page 62, line 19: Ibid, p. 306.

Page 63, line 1: Ibid, p. 309.

Page 64, line 5: Ibid, p. 313.

Page 64, line 13: *We Knew Stonewall Jackson*, p. 59.

Page 69, line 15: Joseph C. Carter and Michael S. Finer. "A survey of leadership: Stonewall Jackson and George S. Patton." *Infantry Magazine*, Jan.-Feb. 2004, v93, i1, p. 10.

Chapter 8

Page 73, line 11: *Life and Letters of "Stonewall" Jackson by His Wife*, p. 283.

Page 74, line 3: "Stonewall Jackson's deadly calm."

Page 74, line 17: *We Knew Stonewall Jackson*, p. 73.

Page 76, line 8: *Stonewall Jackson: The Man, the Soldier, the Legend*, p. 509.

Page 77, line 1: Ibid, p. 568.

Page 79, line 4: http://www.nps.gov/hafe/jackson.htm

Page 80, line 1: *We Knew Stonewall Jackson*, p. 104.

Page 80, line 25: "The Christian Soldier: General Thomas J. 'Stonewall' Jackson."

Page 82, line 8: *We Knew Stonewall Jackson*, p. 111.

Page 82, sidebar: *Life and Letters of "Stonewall" Jackson by His Wife*, p. 377.

Chapter 9

Page 86, line 1: Ibid, p. 423.

Page 86, line 29: http://www.civilwarhome.com/lee2.htm

Page 87, line 2: Ibid.

Page 89, line 1: *We Knew Stonewall Jackson*, p. 123.

Page 90, line 7: Ibid., p. 126.

Page 91, line 21: http://www.nps.gov/frsp/js.htm

Page 91, line 24: "The Christian Soldier: General Thomas J. 'Stonewall' Jackson."

Page 91, line 28: "Thomas Jackson."

Page 91, sidebar: *Stonewall Jackson: The Man, the Soldier, the Legend*, p. 739.

Page 92, line 4: http://www.vmi.edu/archives/manuscripts/ms363009.html

Page 92, line 6: "Stonewall Jackson's deadly calm."

Page 92, line 13: *Stonewall Jackson: The Man, the Soldier, the Legend*, p. 757

Page 92, line 19: "Stonewall Jackson's deadly calm."

Page 95, sidebar: Peter Finn. "Lexington, Va., Bids Fond Farewell to a War Horse." *The Washington Post*, Washington, D.C., Final Edition, July 21, 1997, p. B.01.

Carter, Joseph C., and Michael S. Finer. "A survey of leadership: Stonewall Jackson and George S. Patton." *Infantry Magazine*, Jan.-Feb. 2004, v93, i1.

Cook, Roy Bird. *The Family and Early Life of Stonewall Jackson.* Charleston, W.V.: Education Foundation, Inc., 1967.

Dabney, R.L. *Life and Campaigns of Lieut.-Gen. Thomas J. Jackson.* New York: Blelock, 1866.

Henderson, G.F.R. *Stonewall Jackson and the American Civil War.* New York: Barnes & Noble Books, 1993

Jackson, Mary Anna. *Life and Letters of "Stonewall" Jackson by His Wife.* New York: Harper and Brothers, 1892.

Krick, Robert K. "Stonewall Jackson's deadly calm." *American Heritage,* Dec. 1996, v47, n8.

Krick, Robert K. *Stonewall Jackson at Cedar Mountain.* Chapel Hill: University of North Carolina Press, 1990.

Robertson, James I.. "The Christian Soldier: General Thomas J. 'Stonewall' Jackson." *History Today,* Feb. 2003, v53, i2

Robertson, James I., Jr. *Stonewall Jackson: The Man, the Soldier, the Legend.* New York: Macmillan Publishing, 1997.

Virginia Military Institute. "Stonewall Jackson Resources-VMI Archives." <http://www.vmi.edu/archives/Jackson/Jackson.html>

Wheeler, Richard. *We Knew Stonewall Jackson.* New York: Thomas Y. Crowell Company, 1977.

New York, 18, 29, 30-31
New York, New York, 29, 30-31
North Carolina, 39, 44, 56
Nueces River, 23

Pope, John, 76, 77
Potomac River, 70, 77, 78, 79
Presbyterian Church, 38

Randolph, George Wythe, 67
Rappahanock River, 85
relief sculptures, 12
Richmond, Virginia, 46, 92
Rio Grande, 23
Roman Catholic religion, 27
Romney, Virginia, 61-62, 63, 64

Scott, Winfield, 27
secession, 10, 44
Second Battle of Bull Run, 76-77
Second Corps, 80
Seminole Indians, 33
"Seven Days' Battles," 75
Shenandoah Campaign, 66-70
Shenandoah River, 49, 59
Shenandoah Valley, 59, 60-61, 65
Sherman, William Tecumseh, 22
Shields, James, 67
slavery, 11, 12, 17, 44-45
Smith, James, 88

South Carolina, 10, 44, 53
Spotsylvania National Military Park, 95
Spotsylvania, Virginia, 91, 95
states' rights, 11, 12
Stone Mountain Park, 12
"Stonewall Brigade," 54, 67
Stonewall Jackson Shrine, 95

Tennessee, 44, 62
Texas, 22, 23, 25, 44
tuberculosis, 18
typhoid fever, 15

Utah, 27

Virginia, 9, 10, 12, 15, 36, 44, 45, 46,
    49, 51, 52, 56, 59, 61-62, 62-63,
    67, 70, 71, 74, 76, 78, 79, 81-82,
    85, 90, 91, 95
Virginia Military Institute (VMI),
    36-37, 46, 49, 56, 93, 95

Walker, James A., 37
Warren, Gouverneur K., 92
Washington College, 39
West Point Military Academy, 18-19
Winchester, Virginia, 49, 64-65
Woodson, William Wirt (half-brother),
    16, 18

Robin S. Doak has been writing for children for more than 16 years. A former editor of *Weekly Reader* and *U*S*Kids* magazine, Doak has authored fun and educational materials for kids of all ages. She is a past winner of the Educational Press Association of America Distinguished Achievement Award. She lives with her husband and three children in central Connecticut.

Image Credits

Library of Congress, cover, 2, 4-5, 8, 30, 77, 90, 98 (bottom), 100 (bottom), 101; Stock Montage/Getty Images, 11; Kevin Fleming/Corbis, 13; North Wind Picture Archives, 14, 16, 21, 23, 26, 47, 55, 57, 61, 63, 66, 72, 75, 76, 81, 88, 96 (top); Virginia Military Institute Archives, 17, 28, 36, 39, 40, 48, 83, 93, 97 (top), 98 (top); U.S. Senate Collection/West Point, New York by Seth Eastman, 19; Corbis, 24, 42, 65, 71, 78, 84, 100 (top); Bettmann/Corbis, 32, 45; Medford Historical Society Collection/Corbis, 50, 99; Hulton Archive/Getty Images, 52, 58, 96 (bottom left); MPI/Getty Images, 87; Richard T. Nowitz/Corbis, 94; Texas State Library & Archives Commission, 96 (bottom right); Photodisc, 97 (bottom).

Niles
Public Library District
MAR 2 7 2008
Niles, Illinois 60714

3 1491 00968 5169